MEN-AT-ARMS SERIES

EDITOR: MARTIN WINDROW

Samurai Armies 1550-1615

Text by S. R. TURNBULL

Colour plates by RICHARD HOOK

OSPREY PUBLISHING LONDON

Published in 1979 by
Osprey Publishing Ltd
Member company of the George Philip Group
12–14 Long Acre, London WC2E 9LP
© Copyright 1979 Osprey Publishing Ltd

Reprinted 1980

ISBN 0 85054 302 x

Filmset by BAS Printers Limited,
Over Wallop, Hampshire
Printed in Hong Kong

The author wishes to extend his thanks to Miss
Nahoko Kitagawa, of Osaka University, for help with
translation from Japanese sources.

The Golden Age

The Japanese samurai is usually regarded as being an individual warrior, proud and aloof, to whom personal honour and prowess were of the utmost importance, and who was unwilling to let his achievements be submerged by co-ordinating them with the efforts of others. To some extent the picture is true, at least for the first few centuries of the samurai's existence; but recent research has shown that at the time of the greatest flowering of the samurai spirit, those who actually led the samurai into battle saw their followers in a very different light. This period is the latter half of the 16th and the beginning of the 17th century, the 'Momoyama Period' to historians, although it includes the first few years of the 'Edo Period'. We shall refer to it throughout as the Momoyama Period.

The great generals of Momoyama times thought in terms not of samurai but of samurai armies, where individual prowess was valued in terms of its contribution to a carefully planned strategy involving massive troop movement, wise use of terrain, concentrated firepower, and supplies of food and ammunition assembled on a scale not unlike that of contemporary Europe, and with a degree of skill which contemporary Europe might well have envied.

Since the great Gempei War of 1180–85, Japan had had two rulers: the god-like Emperor in Kyoto, and the military dictator or *Shogun*, in whose hands the Emperor was a mere puppet. However, by 1550

Map of Japan in the Momoyama Period.

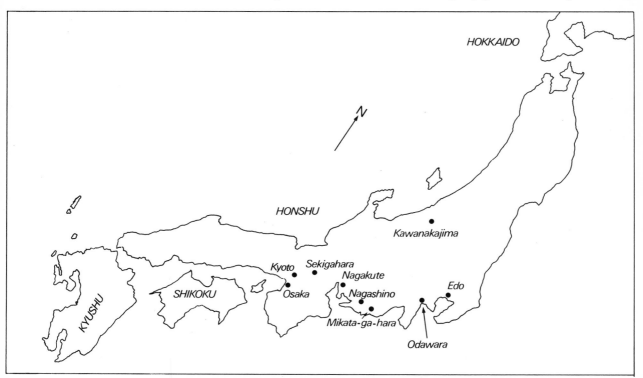

Hanging scroll depicting a samurai of the early sixteenth century.

earnest, and both Takeda and Uesugi used them in their battles. When Takeda Shingen died in 1573 the fortunes of his family fell into the hands of his son Takeda Katsuyori, who inherited an army second to none in the traditional fighting arts. The Takeda samurai were brave and loyal, and renowned for the ferocity of their cavalry charges, while their footsoldiers, too, were disciplined and reliable, in contrast to those of most other daimyo.

In 1575, Takeda Katsuyori came up against one of the greatest original thinkers in the history of the samurai. His name was Oda Nobunaga. The Takeda had long been a threat to the Oda, a threat which came out into the open when Takeda Katsuyori laid siege to an important castle of Nobunaga's called Nagashino. Sensing an opportunity to deal a decisive blow to his enemies, Oda Nobunaga led the relieving force personally, and drew up his army some way from the castle. To deal with the expected Takeda charge, Nobunaga took the finest arquebusiers in his army and arranged them three ranks deep behind a palisade. The results were devastating. One after another the assaults by the Takeda cavalry were blown to smithereens. It was a death blow to the Takeda, and the beginning of a new era in Japanese military history.

The victory of Nagashino showed not only that the firearm had arrived, but also that there was the potential to create an 'army' in the modern sense, for whereas it took long years of practice and highly developed muscles to fire a bow, an ordinary peasant could quickly be taught to fire an arquebus with all the accuracy of which the clumsy weapon was capable. However, Nobunaga also clearly realized, as had Shingen before him, that ordinary peasants were not sufficient to form an army. They had to be trained and organized, given discipline, loyalty, a full belly and a smart uniform. A warlord with these concepts firmly established could think big, in terms of armies of 100,000 men, and even, as events were to prove, of a quarter of a million soldiers fully armed and supplied, to be moved from one end of Japan to the other and across the sea to China.

Where Nobunaga led others followed, but in 1582 Nobunaga, off guard for once in his life, was killed by one of his own generals. Revenge was swift. Toyotomi Hideyoshi, Nobunaga's protégé,

bloody civil war had rendered the office of Shogun as paltry and as powerless as that of the Emperor. Japan was now dotted with what were effectively independent kingdoms, ruled by *daimyo* or barons, all of whom were warriors first and administrators second, and who lived lives of almost constant warfare. Two of the most illustrious of these warlords, Takeda Shingen (1521–73) and Uesugi Kenshin (1530–78), spent over a decade fighting each other at the same place, year after year. Squeezed in beside such Titans were scores of smaller families all engaged in the highly respectable business of stealing each other's land.

Into this turbulent atmosphere in 1543 came three Portuguese merchants, bringing with them the first firearms the Japanese had ever seen: simple matchlock muskets called arquebuses. Within a surprisingly short space of time the samurai had assessed the potential of these weapons, and began producing examples as good as the originals. It was a decisive addition to the Japanese armoury, as for centuries the samurai had fought only with bow, sword and spear.

By 1549 the arquebuses were being used in

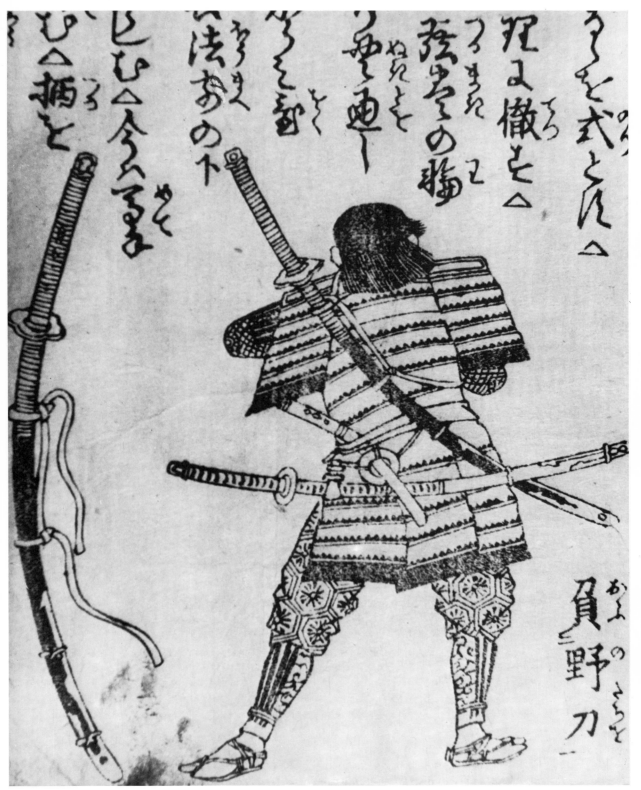

A woodcut depicting a samurai with a *no-dachi* (extra-long sword).

who had begun his career as a sandal bearer, vanquished the usurper within days, and found himself the inheritor of Nobunaga's domain. There were a few rivals to dispose of, whom Hideyoshi defeated with consummate skill in campaigns that depended for their success on the ability to move large numbers of troops quickly around the country while relying on various allies to keep their sectors quiet.

Only one rival proved really troublesome. Tokugawa Ieyasu had fought beside Hideyoshi at Nagashino, and both had learnt its lesson. The result was that in 1584 the two ablest brains among the samurai built defensive earthworks along Komaki hill and settled down to 'trench warfare'. Eventually both sides moved south and fought a pitched battle at Nagakute; Ieyasu won, and then proceeded to ally himself with Hideyoshi.

From then on Hideyoshi went from strength to strength, and one by one the districts of Japan fell to his generalship. The island of Shikoku was first to fall; then Kyushu, ruled by the ancient Shimazu clan; and finally the provinces along the Pacific coast ruled by the Hojo, and the northern estates of the Date family. All were subdued by 1590, when Hideyoshi ascended the tower of Odawara castle and gazed round on a Japan that owed allegiance to none but him. To his ally Tokugawa Ieyasu, a brilliant general and administrator, he gave the castle and town of Edo, which Ieyasu proceeded to make his family seat. How successful he was in this venture may be gathered from the fact that Edo is nowadays called Tokyo.

Meanwhile Hideyoshi planned a campaign that, had it succeeded, might well have changed the course of world history—the conquest of China. In fact the Japanese never got further than that country's border with Korea. For six years the samurai occupied Korean soil, besieging castles and fighting battles with Chinese and Korean armies. The invasion, which had begun so well under fanatical samurai like Kato Kiyomasa (1562–1611), lost its impetus under attack on its lines of communication by the Korean navy. The samurai armies had outreached themselves, and even though nearly 200,000 men had been transported across a hundred miles of sea, the expedition was a failure. In 1596 the samurai returned, tired and dispirited, to a Japan ruled by the five-year-

Armour in *do-maru* style with very large *sode* (shoulder guards).

old son of the late, great Hideyoshi, by whose death the troops had been spared any more foreign service.

Before long the board of regents appointed by Hideyoshi split down the middle, resulting, on 21 October 1600, in the muddy, bloody battle of Sekigahara, the Japanese Culloden. The victor was Tokugawa Ieyasu, Hideyoshi's former ally. It was a victory more complete than any of Hideyoshi's, for by the Battle of Sekigahara Japan gained a Shogun once more, and Shoguns from the Tokugawa family were destined to rule Japan for 250 years.

The army of the Tokugawa, one of the most efficient and modern in Japan, now became the army of the Japanese government. They had, however, one more battle to fight, for the son of Hideyoshi, called Hideyori, was now grown to manhood, and in 1614 he shut himself up in Osaka castle with 60,000 dispossessed and bitter samurai. There followed the most colossal siege in Japanese history, in furtherance of which the Tokugawa tried every trick from bombardment to bribery.

The castle eventually fell in 1615, after a pitched battle outside the castle walls: the last ever large-scale battle between two armies of Japanese samurai.

The notion of a samurai army had now reached a point of perfection from which it could only decline when faced by a situation where wars had virtually ceased. The Shimabara rebellion of 1638 showed how an army could go downhill when there was no need actually to win battles, while old samurai would look back at the glorious days of the Momoyama Period as the golden age of the samurai armies.

Samurai Armies

As the scope and duration of war increased during the 16th century so did the numbers of troops taking part. Documentary evidence relating to the Shimazu clan of Kyushu shows that the mid-16th century showed a dramatic rise in the numbers of soldiers employed in battle, and that even under the straitened circumstances forced upon this particular clan by their defeat at the hands of Hideyoshi in 1587 they were able to supply quite respectably sized armies from 1590 onwards:

Troops fielded by the Shimazu clan, 1411–1614

1411	—Army under Shimazu Motohisa	3,000 men
1484	—Army under Shimazu Takehisa	5,000 men
1576	—Conquest of Northern Kyushu	100,000 men
1576	—Siege of Minamata castle by Shimazu Yoshihisa	115,000 men
1592	—Shimazu contingent sent to the Korean War	15,000 men
1600	—Shimazu at Sekigahara (est.)	12,000 men
1614	—Osaka—winter campaign	10,600 men

Taking into account that battles tended to be fought between alliances of various daimyo, it can be seen that warfare from about 1550 onwards was conducted on a large scale.

The largest increase in the numbers of troops came in the form of lower class warriors, or *ashigaru*. The word itself, which means 'light foot', indicates their original lowly status as absconded peasants or criminal adventurers who joined a feudal army for loot and little else. The samurai had always regarded the use of peasant troops as a necessary evil, provided it did not interfere with their own glorious exploits; but as firearms became generally available they began to give some concern to the welfare of their ashigaru, who now constituted a vital part of their armies. This was no mere philanthropic zeal, but a result of strategic necessity, for whereas the opposing factions in the Gempei War (1180–85) had their home territories situated 300 miles apart from each other, the warring daimyo of the 16th century were all near neighbours. Thus an ashigaru who was not well treated would find it easy to cross a provincial border to till the fields and swell the armies of an enemy.

However, it was a skilful daimyo (Takeda Shingen is one example) who could balance the agricultural and military needs of his provinces. He had to provide the ashigaru with a certain amount of military training without thereby denuding the fields of agricultural workers. The principle on which a successful daimyo was able to operate this division of labour was that one's territory could be defended all year round while agricultural work was continued, but an offensive operation could only be carried out at certain times. Campaigns thus acquired seasons of their own, and would be timed so as to end before winter or a harvest.

A notorious example of the opposite extreme is furnished by Hojo Ujiyasu (1515–70), who issued a call to arms sometime around 1565 which summoned all males between the ages of fifteen and seventy on pain of death, and included the fearsome statement that 'not even a monkey tamer would be let off'.

We are able to estimate the numbers of troops employed in various battles, because those daimyo who were under an obligation to another—and by Hideyoshi's time this included practically everyone—would at certain times be called upon to supply troops for the overlord. The records kept of such musters, from which the following information is taken, give a good insight into the numbers and composition of typical fighting forces of the period, and also enable us to calculate the strength of other daimyos' armies.

In general the number of troops a daimyo—or indeed any landowner, right down to the poorest samurai—was required to supply depended on the wealth of his rice fields, which was measured in *koku*. One koku was supposed to be the amount of rice needed to keep one man for one year.

An early example is the muster of troops by the Shimazu clan at the time of their attack on a fortress called Takabaru in October 1576. Those who owned one *cho* of riceland, yielding about 30 koku, were required to supply two men, that is master and follower. Those holding two cho had to supply three men, master and followers, and so on up to ten cho (300 koku), who would have to supply eleven. They were also expected to bring their own armour, at the ratio of one suit per cho, and thirty days' rice, any who served beyond this time being provided with rice by the lord.

When Hideyoshi invaded Korea in 1592, the daimyo of Kyushu, the island nearest to Korea, had to supply men at the rate of six per hundred koku, with lesser proportions from others according to the distance of their territories from the point of embarkation. At the time of Sekigahara and Osaka the numbers are similar, and work out roughly at two mounted and twenty footsoldiers per 1,000 koku, figures that are supported by the notes of a contemporary European observer. Using this ratio, the contribution of various daimyo at these battles may be estimated. For example, Ii Naotaka, who took a prominent part in the siege of Osaka castle, had a revenue of 10,000 koku in 1610. We may thus expect that the Ii contingent in 1615 would have numbered about twenty mounted and two hundred foot.

As to the distribution of weaponry among these numbers of troops, the muster records are again helpful, such as the data on the siege of Minamata castle by the Shimazu in 1581. This was at the time when this powerful clan was pursuing a vigorous conquest of Kyushu, in the campaign which eventually led to their downfall in 1587:

First encampment: Shimazu Iehisa with 31,000 men including 53 *mono-gashira* (captains)
Second encampment: Shimazu Tadahira with 31,000 men including 51 captains

Main encampment: The commander, Shimazu Yoshihisa, with 53,000 men including 70 captains

Details are then given of Yoshihisa's personal force:

Officers and messengers (listed by name).

Ashigaru:
100 spearmen, of whom 10 are substitutes, with a samurai (not mounted) between 10 spearmen; under 2 spear *bugyo* (commissioners, in other words officers in charge of the spearmen); 100 archers, of whom 10 are substitutes, with a samuarai (not mounted) between 10 archers, under 2 arrow commissioners; 100 arquebusiers, of whom 10 are substitutes, with a samurai (not mounted) between 10, under 2 gun commissioners

General staff:
3 war commissioners with 30 men each
2 standard commissioners
3 ensigns with 60 men
4 commissioners for works with 12 men
4 commissioners for horses, with men

Personal staff:
Lord's attendants: 20 men including 4 in charge of luggage
In charge of the lord's treasury: 6 mounted men
60 footsoldiers
60 *komono* (pages)
2 hat-bearers
2 staff-bearers
12 general bearers
3 chests of armour, 9 men to carry
3 horses, 2 saddled, one unsaddled, 15 grooms
3 sandal-bearers

The lord's weapons:
3 bows, 3 men to carry
3 quivers, 6 men to carry
2 *naginata* (glaives), 3 men to carry
2 spears, 3 men to carry
2 *no-dachi* (extra-long swords), 3 men to carry
3 *katana* (long swords), 3 men to carry
1 *wakizashi* (short sword), 3 men to carry

Domestic staff:
2 culinary officials with 35 men, including 9

firemakers, 2 rice cooks, 6 stable boys and 9 labourers.

Forty years later, Shimazu Iehisa, Yoshihisa's nephew, sent an army to fight for the Tokugawa at the siege of Osaka castle. The numbers are much smaller, and we do not have the same detailed records of the commander's personal retinue. The army, as of 20 January 1614, consisted of three contingents totalling 10,300 men, with 187 *nobori* (long vertical flags bearing the Shimazu *mon*, or badge, of a black cross in a ring), plus 289 mounted samurai.

Included in the 10,300 were 750 labourers plus a baggage train of 300 men with pack horses.

The personal guard of Shimazu Iehisa:
Bodyguard: 456 dismounted, 130 mounted samurai
300 arquebusiers
200 archers
200 spearmen
56 banners
50 shield-bearers with shields
30 chests of armour
30 loads of 100 arrows, each carried by one man
30 loads of bullet and powder (for the arquebus corps), one load per man
50 loads of gunpowder (50,000 shots), one load per man
Weapon-bearers to the lord's attendants (number unspecified)
15 horses

It is interesting to note the increased reliance put on the firearm compared with 1581. This shift in emphasis is supported by the data for the Shimazu contingent for Korea in 1592, which included 1,500 arquebuses, 1,500 bows and 300 spears; and a reinforcement sent by Date Masamune to Tokugawa Ieyasu in October 1600 which included 1,200 arquebuses, 850 spears and 200 bows, plus 330 unspecified personnel such as baggage carriers.

The most detailed breakdown of weaponry comes from after the establishment of the Tokugawa Shogunate in 1603. From this time forward the Tokugawa clan army became the army of the Shogunate, and thus in effect the standing army of the Japanese nation. This meant that all samurai were theoretically part of this huge army, and would be required to supply men and materials for it according to schedules not dissimilar from those described above. At the same time a daimyo was officially defined as a samurai having an income of 10,000 koku and over, while below this level samurai were divided into *hatamoto* (bannermen, basically 'leaders') having an income of between 100 koku and 9,500 koku, or *go-kenin* (housemen, basically 'followers') having an income of below 100 koku.

Daimyo and bannermen were required to provide housemen and footsoldiers according to the schedules, which were revised slightly over the years, the final revision of 1649 lasting until the mid-19th century. A couple of examples will suffice to show how it operated. They are taken from the 1649 revision, but it is unlikely that previous lists were much different:

Bannerman samurai, income 300 koku:
Personal service, plus:
1 samurai (houseman)
1 spearman
1 armour-bearer
1 groom
1 sandal-bearer
1 *hasamibako*-bearer (this was a travelling case carried on a pole)
1 baggage carrier

Bannerman samurai, income 2,000 koku:
Personal service, plus:
8 samurai (housemen)
2 armour-bearers plus 1 reserve
5 spearmen plus 1 reserve
4 grooms
4 baggage carriers
1 sandal-bearer
2 hasamibako-bearers plus 1 reserve
1 archer
2 arquebusiers
2 fodder-bearers
1 no-dachi-bearer
2 ashigaru leaders
1 rain-hat carrier

All the soldiers in apparently non-combatant rôles would be fully armed and ready for action.

Schedules for higher income groups (3,000 koku and over) included non-armoured servants (*wakato*) and pages (komono).

As well as the levies provided by the schedules, there were also several 'regular' corps in the Tokugawa army, of which the élite was the *O-ban*, or Great Guard. It had existed since Ieyasu's early campaigns, and had originally consisted of three companies, increased to five in 1592 and to twelve in 1623. In each company were fifty guardsmen under one captain and four *kumi-gashira* (lieutenants). The numbers were swelled by the troops which each member of the Guard had to furnish according to the schedule of incomes.

An interesting specialist corps in the Tokugawa army, which certainly existed in 1575 and possibly earlier, was the *utsukai-ban* or 'honourable messenger corps'. Originally numbering twenty-eight in all, these men wore a *sashimono* (the banner on the back of a suit of armour) bearing the character *go*, meaning 'five'.

From 1603 onwards a number of other corps were introduced, mainly concerned with the guarding of various fortresses of the Tokugawa, such as Edo and Nagoya.

Samurai Battles

In the traditional samurai battle described in the ancient epics, proceedings would begin with a duel of arrows, followed by challenges to individual combat. By the 16th century, however, such niceties had been abandoned, and the experience of centuries of warfare had evolved into some degree of set strategy and tactics. Much of the credit must go to Takeda Shingen and Uesugi Kenshin, whose periodic battles of Kawanakajima (fights are recorded for 1553, 1554, 1555, 1556, 1557 and 1563) were often little more than exercises in troop movement. By the time that Shingen and Kenshin were engaged in real, bloody battles with generals of the calibre of Nobunaga and Ieyasu, both sides could adopt certain tactical dispositions, familiar and tried, adapted to the circumstances in which the commanders found themselves.

The most significant development in tactics in the Momoyama Period was in the field of firearms,

particularly in the form of volley firing which had proved to be so effective in the Battle of Nagashino. From then on the arquebusiers formed the front ranks of most armies, with spearmen as a guard, and archers as skirmishers, sharpshooters, and as rank firers between rows of arquebusiers to keep the enemies' heads down while the guns were being reloaded.

Certain standard battle formations were worked out, most of which had poetic names. A selection are illustrated in the accompanying diagrams.

(1) *Ganko* ('birds in flight'). This is a flexible arrangement of troops which can easily be changed as the situation develops. A solid screen of arquebusiers protects the front and rear, but there are sufficient on the flanks to move round should the enemy alter his dispositions. The general is situated to the rear, but near to the centre so that communication is not lost.

(2) *Hoshi* ('arrowhead'). This is the formation for a fierce charge, in classic Japanese style. A thinner screen of arquebuses lead the vanguard samurai, who will swoop into the gaps left by the arquebus casualties in the enemy's ranks. As this is a highly mobile formation, the drums and other signalling devices are hedged round by the lord's personal retainers. The arrowhead was designed for rapid penetration, so the flanks are but lightly protected by bows and spears.

(3) *Saku* ('keyhole'). This was regarded as being the best defence against the 'arrowhead'. Six ranks of arquebuses, supported by two ranks of bows, are angled to receive the 'arrowhead' attack into them and to meet it with crossfire. The samurai form the shape of a keyhole around the general, to withstand the shock of the charge.

(4) *Kakuyoku* ('crane's wing'). The best formation for surrounding your enemy. Again the arquebuses and bows soften the enemy up, followed by the vanguard samurai who engage the enemy in hand-to-hand fighting while the second company spreads out to envelop them. Note how the shape of the second company's formation, being convexly curved, does not suggest to an enemy an immediate threat of being surrounded. Indeed, from the front

Battle formations of the Momoyama and Edo Periods (for description see text).

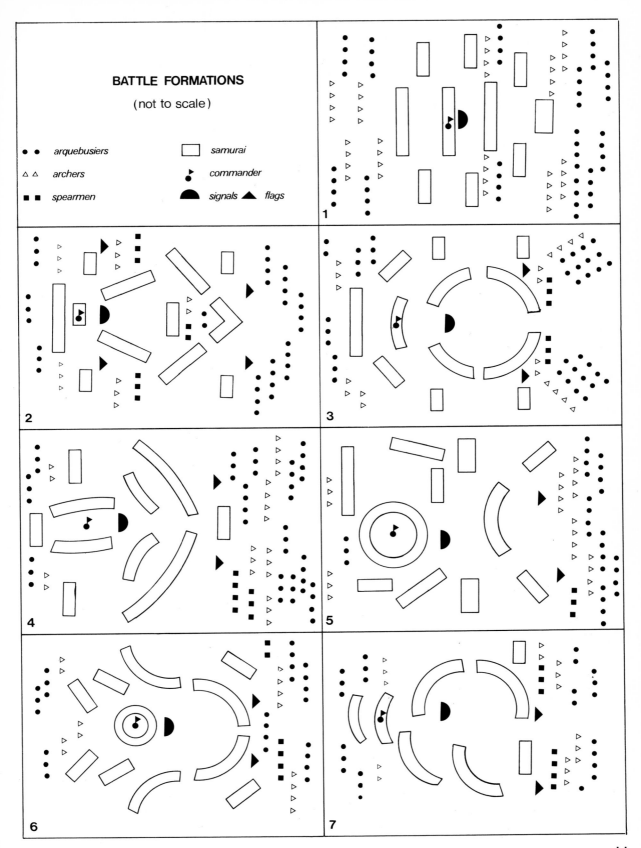

BATTLE FORMATIONS

(not to scale)

• • arquebusiers   ▭ samurai

△ △ archers   ◗ commander

■ ■ spearmen   ◖ signals ▲ flags

an 'arrowhead' might be expected, which would be exactly what a general would want his enemy to think.

(5) *Koyaku* ('yoke'). This formation is so called from a fanciful resemblance to the yoke round the necks of oxen. It was a flexible defence, ideally against a 'crane's wing' but equally effective against an 'arrowhead'. The split vanguard could absorb a frontal attack long enough for the enemy's intentions to be made evident. The second and third companies could then react accordingly, either forming a 'keyhole' against an 'arrowhead', or spreading out to avoid envelopment.

(6) *Gyorin* ('fish scales'). This formation is the one to adopt if you have an army that is outnumbered by your enemy's and you wish to break his ranks in true samurai fashion. It is basically a blunted 'arrowhead' for a force that has not the power to risk all in a fierce charge, but must rather maintain sustained pressure against one sector. Its name is an allusion to the shape formed by the vanguard and second company.

(7) *Engetsu* ('half moon'). This is for a 'backs to the wall' situation. The army has not been surrounded, but owing to heavy losses there is great likelihood of this happening. The broken corps are pulled back, and the vanguard and other companies form a half moon that can be adapted as the situation develops. The arquebusiers arrange themselves in depth with a long rank of spearmen and archers behind.

There are many others, mainly variations of those described above. The 'tiger's head' is a modified 'birds in flight' for an army of about half the size. The 'long snake' provides for attack from both sides, while the 'lying dragon' is the form of 'tiger's head' to adopt when on top of a hill.

It was a measure of a general's skill as to how long he could hold his troops in formations such as those described above before the samurai spirit asserted itself and they started fighting the enemy of their own accord. During the Summer campaign of Osaka in 1615, the Osaka garrison, largely composed of *ronin* (dispossessed samurai) took up positions opposite the great Tokugawa army. Several ronin in the front ranks began blazing away with their arquebuses, in spite of commands to stop

lest a premature attack spoil the carefully planned encircling movement that was unfolding at the rear.

It was not just irregular troops who made the conduct of a battle sometimes difficult to control. The old samurai ethic of individual glory at all costs was as attractive as it had ever been. In particular, great store was laid on being the first into battle, and there are numerous examples of samurai impetuosity almost ruining well-laid plans. The most notorious example is probably the disgraceful conduct of Fukushima Masanori and Ikeda Terumasa in 1600. Ieyasu had despatched them with their armies to secure the castle of Gifu, which controlled the two main roads from Ieyasu's capital of Edo (Tokyo) to the west. It was vital for the success of Ieyasu's plans in the campaign that culminated in Sekigahara that Gifu be captured speedily. Instead, Ikeda and Fukushima quarrelled about precedence, and were even ready to fight a duel over the matter when common sense prevailed in the form of a compromise: so Fukushima attacked the front, while Ikeda simultaneously attacked the back.

Besides such uniquely Japanese problems, a general was faced with the common difficulty of all armies—that of communication. Tokugawa Ieyasu once remarked:

'It is a mistake to think that battles can be won by sitting on a camp stool giving orders, baton in hand, as is the way of many. . . . A commander will not conquer by gazing at men's backs. In a fight the best thing is to charge with the greatest vigour. . . .'

Ieyasu certainly seems to have taken a more active part in his battles than a lot of his contemporaries, and usually commanded from horseback. An observer remarked that he would begin quietly enough, directing the troops with his baton, but as the fight developed he would become very excited and hammer on the pommel of his saddle with his fists, shouting, 'Kakare! Kakare!' ('At them! At them!'). At Osaka, his last battle, fought at the age of seventy-three, he was so close to the action that he is believed to have been wounded near the kidneys by a spear.

Visible signals given by generals, and indeed all samurai in positions of command, were indicated by waving some form of commander's baton. A general would use a *saihai*, which was a short staff with a tassel of leather or paper suspended from the end. Alternatively the batons would take the form of fans. The *uchiwa*, used today by referees of sumo wrestling, were rigid and shaped like a figure of eight. Lower-ranking officers would carry a *tetsuten*, which looks and works like an ordinary fan except that the outer sticks, and sometimes all the sticks, are made of metal. They were covered with parchment and bore the rising sun as a decoration on a contrasting ground colour. Combinations of black, red and gold were popular.

Audible commands were carried by drums, conch-shell trumpets, and gongs.

The commander would set up his headquarters in some convenient position, such as the top of a hill. The headquarters would be screened from view by the *maku*—curtains as high as a man, suspended from cords looped between posts sunk into the ground. The maku usually bore the commander's mon, or badge, painted large. At the conclusion of a successful battle the victorious commander would sit within the maku for the bizarre ceremony of viewing the heads. For centuries, the taking of an enemy's head had been regarded as the best proof of a job well done, and by Momoyama times the affair had attained ritualistic proportions. The commander would attire himself in full armour and sit on his lacquered camp stool, often covered with a bear or tiger skin, with his saihai or uchiwa in his hand. Samurai would then bring him the heads of illustrious personages, which the commander would examine and comment upon. Before presentation each head would be washed, the hair combed, and the whole grisly trophy mounted on a square wooden board with a spike in the middle to hold it securely. The head would be carried by a footsoldier, and if there was a shortage of wooden boards then a war fan would suffice, with a few leaves to dry up the blood. A label attached to the pigtail gave the name of the samurai whose trophy it was.

Even commanders of the quality of Ieyasu were superstitious, and great believers in lucky omens. Centuries before, commanders would have refused to attack from certain directions that were regarded as being unlucky on that particular day, and remnants of this belief still persisted. An old tradition among the samurai was the eating of the three lucky dishes before going into battle. The three foods—dried *awabi* (a shellfish), *kombu* (seaweed), and chestnuts—were served on a lacquered tray along with *sake* (rice wine), as a way of bringing good luck to the warrior.

If the nature of a pitched battle precluded any very tight discipline being exerted on the soldiery, such hindrances were absent when on the march, and in this instance a great measure of order and control would be exacted. Interesting evidence is provided by Ieyasu's field orders for the Odawara campaign of 1590:

'1. If anyone advances or reconnoitres without orders he shall be punished.

2. Anyone who advances too far, even to gain glory, will be punished.

3. Anyone who trespasses in another company without proper reason will be deprived of his horse and arms.

4. When troops are on the march none shall go by by-ways. If any move in a disorderly fashion their leader will be held responsible.

5. Anyone who disobeys the orders of the bugyo (commissioners) will be punished.

6. When troops are on the march all flags, guns, bows and spears are to be carried according to fixed order. All will march at the command of the commissioner.

[It is interesting to speculate what these "fixed orders" were. The arquebuses were carried at the slope, barrel uppermost, on the right shoulder, and spears probably the same way.]

7. Except when in the ranks it is forbidden to go about carrying long spears.

8. Anyone letting a horse stray in the camp will be punished.

9. As to the baggage train, strict orders are to be given that they are to be allotted a proper place so that they do not get mixed up with the troops. Any who do so will be put to death on the spot. [Note that this is the first offence to carry a death penalty warning.]

10. Without orders no one may seize any man or woman and take them. The vanguard shall not, without orders, set fire to any house in enemy territory.

11. Violence and intimidation of tradespeople is strictly forbidden. Offenders will be put to death on the spot.

12. Anyone who strikes camp without orders will be punished.'

An army on the march must have been a stirring sight. When Hideyoshi set off to fight the Odawara campaign, the streets of Kyoto were thronged with people. Wooden stands were erected so that they could get a good view of the master of propaganda. In his more modest days, when he set off in 1578 to chastise the Mori clan on Nobunaga's behalf, the army was recorded as it left Kyoto for the west. The order of marching was as follows:

1. Flag-bearers
2. Arquebusiers
3. Archers
4. Spearmen
5. Samurai on foot
6. Mounted samurai
7. Wardrum, conch and gong
8. Samurai commissioners
9. Hideyoshi himself, preceded by a spare horse, armour-bearer and servants, and followed by a helmet carrier
10. More samurai
11. Flag-bearers

Sieges

To appreciate the techniques of siegework used in Japan it is necessary to understand something of the nature of the Japanese castle. Fortified positions began to be used in large numbers in the 14th century, when generals like Kusunoki Masashige defended wooden stockades. The art of castle building really got under way in the 16th century, the impetus for their construction being the introduction of firearms. This is in direct contrast to the experience of contemporary Europe, where the use of gunpowder signalled the death knell of castle building. The difference was that the Japanese, as we shall see, never developed cannon to any great degree, so castles were seen merely as defence against arquebus fire and cavalry charges.

To some extent castles were a natural evolution, using stone as an extra building material, from the earlier fortified stockade. Castles tended to be built on hills, and if there was no hill available then a mound would be excavated which would be faced with huge blocks of dressed stone. This gave the castle walls a characteristically curved shape, which may have helped somewhat to cushion the impact of the frequent earth tremors felt in Japan, but also provided a good surface for attackers to scale.

A castle was also the perfect base for a garrison, in a style of warfare that required troops to be ready at various parts of the country. Finally, it served as a symbol of a lord's wealth and pride, and no one understood this better than Nobunaga whose fortress of Azuchi, the first castle to have a tower keep, set a grand style that Hideyoshi was to copy at Osaka and Ieyasu at Edo.

Japanese castles can be regarded as being composed of two separate parts. The massive stone walls surrounded by moats remind us of an English castle, but there the resemblance ends. Within the walls are various buildings, all of pure Japanese design. These superstructures are built of wood, and in later examples are raised on stone-covered mounds in the form of keeps. Their apparent flimsiness makes a stark contrast to the solidity of the stone beneath, and begs the question of fire, for once the outer walls had been breached an attacker could easily set fire to the keep and subsidiary buildings.

The Japanese response to this danger was to build the wooden structures within a series of vast baileys. As the Japanese lacked the means to deliver fire from a great distance, the attacker was given no advantage by the building's materials.

The most popular, if not the most successful technique for attacking a castle was by direct assault against the walls or gates. This could be very costly in men and materials, as the defenders would line the walls with arquebusiers and pick off attackers as they clambered up. Alternatively the garrison could withdraw within the walls (as they did at Osaka in 1614), form ranks, and fire volleys at the attacking samurai as they appeared over the walls. If an assault succeeded it was only by sheer weight of numbers, as was the case in the Korean War when one fortress after another fell to the fanatical Japanese. At Tong-nai the leader of the army, Konishi Yukinaga, was the first to mount the bamboo scaling ladders set up against the wall.

The experience of the Korean War, particularly the latter part of it when the Korean castles were defended by Chinese troops, led to many advances in siege warfare. Mining a castle had been well established since Hideyoshi's first successful use of it

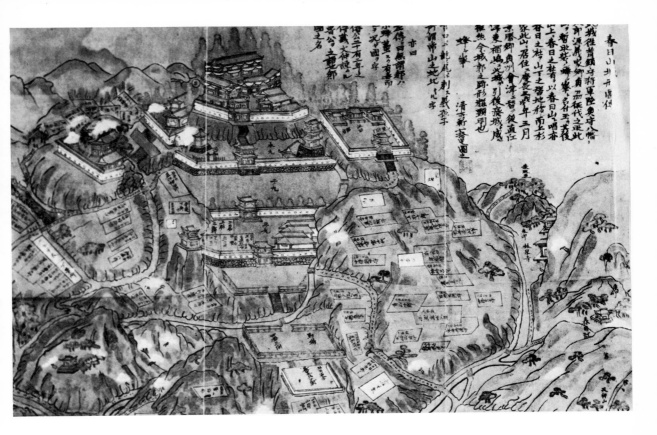

against the fortress of Kameyama in 1583. The use
of a moat would effectively block mining, but on
one occasion Hideyoshi was able to turn this
defensive technique into an offensive one. He
noticed that the castle of Takamatsu was built on
low ground within a valley, near which flowed a
river. Turning his entire army into one vast
engineer force, Hideyoshi managed to dam the
river and divert its flow into the valley. As the water
level began to creep up the walls of the castle
Hideyoshi kept up a bombardment with heavy
calibre muskets until the commander eventually
surrendered.

The progress of an attacker could further be
hindered by the use of obstacles. Metal caltrops,
spiked tetrahedra that always fell with one spike
pointing upwards, were very effective against feet
wearing only straw sandals. Trees would be cut
down with their branches pointing towards the
enemy, and particularly nasty obstacles could be
provided by simple lengths of bamboo stuck in the
ground at an angle with the ends cut off diagonally,
giving a surprisingly sharp point. Short stakes
hammered into the ground with ropes tied from one

Old print showing Kasuga-yama castle, built by Uesugi Kenshin (1530–78).

stake to another provided the 16th-century equiva-
lent of barbed wire entanglements. All obstacles
had the same purpose: to inflict harm if that was
possible, but mainly to hinder the attackers'
progress towards the walls, so that they would
provide a better target for the arquebus volley and
the sharpshooters with bows.

Kato Kiyomasa is credited with several advances
in siege techniques pioneered during the Korean
War. During one attack on a Chinese fortress that
had a deep dry moat, Kiyomasa ordered all his
soldiery to go into the fields and cut the ripe and
juicy rice stalks and bind them into bundles.
During the night the samurai tossed these bundles
into the moat, making a pile so high that it nearly
reached the level of the walls. While arquebusiers
in the ranks kept the defenders' heads down, a band
of determined samurai scaled the walls and
overpowered the garrison.

Another of Kiyomasa's inventions was the
'tortoise shell wagon' a rough wagon on wheels

which could be pushed to the walls. It was protected from above by hides hardened in a fire. Under this roof footsoldiers would prise away the stones of the wall to make a breach.

If it was clear that an assault was not going to be immediately successful then the attacking commander would prepare to starve the defenders out. Elaborate preparations were made to conduct a siege of this type. The castle would first be sealed off from the outside world by building a fence or palisade all round it, usually consisting of bundles of bamboo tied to a wooden framework. If the castle stood on a river then a chain boom would be put across it, and a guard ship would be floated if the river entered the sea nearby. At intervals along the palisade a siege tower would be erected so that the attacking commander could see into the castle. Siege towers ranged from a simple four-sided ladder to quite a solid-looking affair with a wooden lookout post on top, such as Ieyasu used against Osaka. An interesting variation, attributed to Takeda Shingen's celebrated general Yamamoto Kansuke, consisted of a platform on wheels supporting a high wooden framework with a pulley attached. The samurai who wished to observe was placed in a wooden box and hauled up to the top by a rope. No doubt he was speedily brought down again if the sector got too 'hot', as any sign of life round a siege tower was a signal to a garrison to blaze away at it with everything they possessed.

The Japanese also invented a mobile variation of the usually fixed wooden shield. There were two types, one of wood and the other of bundles of bamboo, both with weapon slits cut through, which the soldiers could push towards the castle to provide covering fire for an assault party, or to get closer range for a sniper.

Bribery was so common a device in siegework as to make it almost respectable. Arson was the usual service a traitor could perform on an attacker's behalf.

As previously indicated, the Japanese never really developed the making and use of cannon. They certainly appreciated their potential, for they suffered heavily from the Korean superiority in these matters, but Japanese casting techniques were never sufficiently good to produce cannon of anything like the quality they were able to obtain from the Europeans. Whenever a foreign ship arrived, negotiations began for its armament. For example, the Dutch ship that brought Will Adams (the first Englishman to visit Japan) in 1600 had its cargo impounded by Ieyasu. This was shortly before Sekigahara, but none of the guns was used at that battle, or indeed in any field battle of the time. This was because all the cannon had been made for ships, and thus what the Japanese removed from the ship consisted of little more than the barrel. As wheeled transport of any sort was rarely used, all war materials had to be lugged from place to place by man or horse, or conveyed by ship along the coasts and river estuaries. Consequently there was no such thing as a field battery in Momoyama Japan, and what cannon were used were confined to siege-work.

It is sometimes difficult to deduce from contemporary descriptions of firearms heavier than an arquebus whether the observer is indicating cannon or one of the varieties of heavy calibre musket called wall guns. A wall gun was basically a large arquebus, fired when resting on a wall or similar support. (The Japanese never used the hand-held 'rest' employed by European musketeers.) One wall gun, used by the Tokugawa when besieging Osaka castle, is still preserved. It weighs 135 kilogrammes and is 3 metres long. It was made in 1610.

Actual cannon were used both by besiegers and besieged at Osaka. One used by the defenders is preserved in Japan. It has a calibre of 90 millimetres, is 2·9 metres long, and fired an 8-pound shot. Since all that is left is the barrel, it is impossible to say how it was mounted for service. Probably some form of wooden support would have been used, but recoil must have been a problem. There is an interesting contemporary painted scroll which shows a cannon being fired from the battlements. It appears to be resting on nothing but a pile of rice-bales, while a group of ashigaru sit around it expectantly.

Sometimes cannon were raised up into siege towers to bombard a castle from a height—such a hazardous business for the gunners that wall guns must be implied, rather than actual cannon. Ieyasu used heavy bombardment of Osaka as a weapon of psychological warfare.

As to the size of cannon used, we may note that the usual armament for an English ship of the period was a culverin, firing an 18-pound shot, or a saker, firing a 5-pound shot, so we may assume that the cannon available to the Japanese were within the limits of these weights. In 1615, after the fall of Osaka, Tokugawa Hidetada was presented by the Dutch with two sakers.

In addition to cannon, a form of fire-projecting mangonel was used. It was a simple catapult that fired a bomb with a lighted fuse. Kobayakawa Takakage is known to have used one, which dates its early use to about 1580–90. Similar models were used at Osaka.

Dress and Equipment: Samurai

Peace

The clothes a samurai would wear when not actually prepared to fight a battle, that is when not in armour, would depend upon the degree of formality of the occasion. The basic male dress was the *kimono*, a long, wide-sleeved garment like a dressing-gown, reaching to well below the knee, sometimes worn over a similarly shaped white undergarment that showed at the neck. It would be held in at the waist by a long sash-like belt which was wrapped round two or three times before being tied at the front. Into this belt the samurai thrust his swords.

The kimono would suffice the samurai if he was off to enjoy himself on a summer's evening, and probably all he would wear under it would be a *fundoshi*, or loincloth. Otherwise he would wear in addition a pair of *hakama*, or wide trousers. The hakama were rather like a divided skirt. They were stiffened and had a low crotch with large openings at the sides, and were held in place by two sets of ties on the front and rear parts, fastening round the waist. The hakama came to the ankle, and when wearing them the swords would still be carried in the kimono belt but outside the hakama.

The *daisho* (pair of swords) was the mark of the samurai. The larger, called the *katana*, was the standard fighting sword, and for a well-to-do samurai this would be of exceptional workmanship and was often a treasured possession or heirloom. The blade of the sword was slightly curved, making

it ideal as a cutting and slashing weapon in the two-handed Japanese style. Along the blade of the best examples could be discerned a wavy temper line where the hard steel of the cutting edge met and was surrounded by the softer steel of the sword body, giving strength and springiness. The tang of the blade fitted tightly into the wooden handle, which was covered in *same*, the skin of the giant ray,

Samurai wearing a suit of armour typical of the practical styles of the Momoyama Period.

The standard fighting sword, or *katana*.

and then bound tightly with dark-blue silk braid to give a firm grip. A small round *tsuba*, or sword-guard, was fitted where the blade entered the hilt. The scabbard would probably be lacquered, and would bear on it a small projection through which the *sageo*, a silken cord, was passed to make the scabbard fast in the belt.

The short sword (wakizashi) would be of identical style. Both were carried with the cutting edge uppermost so that a deadly blow could be delivered direct from the scabbard.

The samurai had to be ready to fight at a moment's notice, and when danger threatened he would speedily prepare his loose and awkward clothing for the fray. The hakama would be hitched up inside the belt, while the sleeves would be tied up with the *tasuki*, a narrow sash, which was passed in front of the arms and crossed on the back. An experienced samurai could perform both tasks in a few seconds.

On his feet the samurai would wear the divided socks called *tabi*, which will be described in the section on armour. The tabi in 'civilian dress' were often white, and might be omitted altogether in summer, but a samurai would never go barefoot out of doors. He would usually wear straw sandals, or even a pair of *geta*, wooden clogs with supports for raising them off the ground. Geta would never be worn when there was a chance of danger, as they were too clumsy for swift movement.

For more formal occasions, such as guard duty at a castle, the samurai would augment the hakama with a *kataginu*, making a combination called the *kami-shimo* (upper-lower). The kataginu was a curious form of jacket with no sleeves, in which the

shoulders and back were quilted and stiffened so that they stood out like wings. The kataginu would be of the same colour and pattern as the hakama. A decorative feature of the kami-shimo was the use of the mon, the lord's heraldic device, which was placed on the front straps of the kataginu, the middle of the back, the sleeves of the kimono when worn under kami-shimo, and the top rear of the hakama.

Warrior wearing *kamishimo*, the combination of *hakama* (trousers) and *kataginu* (jacket).

18

For very formal occasions in the Edo Period, such as presentation to the Shogun, very high-ranking samurai would be expected to wear the *naga-bakama*, extremely long trousers that trailed on the floor behind the wearer and completely enclosed his feet. It was a mark of good breeding to be able to move in them, a task which required supreme co-ordination. It also ensured that a samurai wearing naga-bakama would find it impossible to perform an assassination, or at least to get away afterwards.

The samurai changed his dress when going on a journey, for example the regular trips to Edo to visit the Shogun that began in the early years of the Edo Period. The hakama were perfectly suitable for a mounted man, but he would change his kataginu for a *haori*, which was a three-quarter length kimono-shaped coat. Those on foot wore the haori over a different pair of trousers, narrower than the hakama and tucked into gaiters. The tail of the haori was draped over the sword scabbards, giving the samurai a characteristic silhouette as he walked along.

Headgear consisted of a large straw hat called a *kasa*, similar to that worn by Japanese country folk to this day, which served as a protection against both sun and rain. A deeper version, looking rather like a waste-paper basket, covered the entire head, leaving a gap at the front through which the wearer could see. It was a useful thing for a samurai to wear if he did not wish to be recognized, such as on a clandestine visit to the pleasure quarters of Edo. An alternative was a cloth cap or hood, which was also useful on cold days.

A samurai who had become dispossessed owing to the death or degradation of his master was called a ronin, a name which means 'man of the waves', because they wandered from place to place seeking employment for their swords. Needless to say the ronin wore whatever he could get, including armour. Thousands of ronin packed the walls of Osaka castle during the great sieges of 1614 and 1615, hoping to revenge their late masters on the Tokugawa family. The 'Seven Samurai' in the famous film are all ronin.

The *ninja*, the specially trained spies and assassins used by the daimyos, were garbed from head to foot in black. The jacket was similar to a modern judo jacket in shape, while a black hood completely enclosed the head, leaving a gap only for the eyes.

Warrior wearing *kamishimo*, and carrying the two swords.

Tight trousers tucked into gaiters over black socks, and even the straw sandals were black and specially padded so that the ninja could walk noiselessly.

An important aspect of any samurai's appearance was the dressing of the hair, upon which much care and attention was lavished. Even a ronin would take some pride in this aspect of his toilet, and to an ordinary samurai, having a single hair out of place was a disgrace. It had become customary during the early 16th century to shave off the hair from the front part of the head. This had originally been for the sake of comfort when wearing a helmet, but by Momoyama times it had become a mere whim of fashion. The tonsured

Samurai hairstyles, showing the queue, one with the *sakayaki* (tonsure) and one without.

portion of the head was called the *sakayaki*, and what hair remained was drawn back into a queue on the back of the head. There were two methods of making this queue. One was called *chasen-gami*, because of a fanciful resemblance to the bamboo tea-whisk used in the Japanese tea ceremony. It involved coiling a piece of string round and round the lower half of the tuft so as to make it stick out like a shaving brush. The other style, far more common, was to gather the oiled hair into a long narrow cylindrical queue at the back, bend it forward and then back again, and tie it in place. This style, called *mitsu-ori*, or threefold, was popular in the Momoyama Period.

A variation on this style, which became popular later, was the *futatsu-ori*, or two-fold, where the queue was bent forward only, over the sakayaki. The end of the queue, however it was made, would be neatly trimmed with a razor.

Young samurai were an exception to the above fashion. Their tonsure extended only to shaving the forepart of the crown, so that the forelock itself was left intact. This unshaven forelock was trimmed to make a triangular shape which was combed backwards. The illustration on page 21 shows Honda Tadakatsu (1548–1610) as a young man wearing this hairstyle.

Not all samurai followed the fashion for shaving the forepart of the head, and would form the queue from the full head of hair pulled back. Tokugawa Ieyasu was vehemently against it, as he said the shaving spoiled the look of a head when it was cut off. Ieyasu was quite a connoisseur of heads, and impressed on his men that before they went into battle they should perfume their hair by burning incense below it.

When armour was worn the queue was untied and the hair combed back: hence the romantic

Young warrior wearing the young man's version of the samurai hairstyle.

19th-century prints of samurai with their hair streaming in the wind.

Samurai who were also Buddhist monks would have their entire heads shaven.

War

The basis of samurai equipment in war, which occupied a great deal of time in the period under discussion, was the suit of armour. As this was an age when the nature of warfare was changing rapidly, so too the suit of armour underwent many changes in its design and efficiency.

Up to the 13th century there had been two distinct types of armour: the *yoroi*, a heavy, box-like and very ornate style for the mounted samurai, and the *do-maru*, a simple suit of armour for the footsoldier, which was wrapped round the body and fastened at the side. Both were constructed from small metal plates called *kozane* laced to-

gether, side by side, with leather. The strips so formed were then lacquered to guard against rust, and a series were tied together with silk cords to make a light but resilient armour plate. A do-maru would consist of one big sheet of these kozane with a divided skirt (*kusazuri*) and some means of suspending the whole from the shoulders and fastening it.

During the 14th century, however, when the samurai were faced with the task of defending outposts, and other modes of warfare where the horse need only be regarded as a means of transport to a battlefield, they began to see in the humble do-maru a lighter and more convenient suit of armour than the bulky and heavy yoroi. The do-maru thus became samurai armour as well, and a variant on it was developed, called the *haramaki*, which opened at the back.

During the 15th and early 16th centuries campaigns became of increasingly longer duration, so the samurai was forced actually to wear his armour for extremely long periods without rest. The armour-makers therefore turned their attentions to the comfort of their clients by considering the distribution of the armour's weight, for the do-maru, although easier to wear than the old yoroi, still had the disadvantage that its whole weight was borne on the shoulders. The design was therefore modified by tapering the body of the do-maru in towards the waist, so that at least some of the weight was taken on the hips rather than on the shoulders. This style, the *tachi-do*, led to the characteristic shape of the armours of the Momoyama Period.

The armour-makers then began thinking about the actual construction of the armour itself. The kozane style, in which the horizontal strips were made up of many small plates, had the grave disadvantage that each scale had no fewer than fourteen holes, with a consequent weakening of the metal. Also, the resulting system of lacing the horizontal strips together with numerous cords, called *kebiki-odoshi*, had several disadvantages when on campaign. The mass of braid would absorb water during a rainstorm, with a resulting increase in the weight to be carried. In winter a sodden do-maru might well freeze solid, while during a long and hot summer campaign the lacing would become muddy and evil-smelling, and provide a refuge for ants and lice detrimental to the health of the wearer. Finally, a heavily laced *do* (do being the waist with the body of the do, the lowest circumference of the kusazuri being identical with the circumference of the do at the breast.

Two styles of this *tosei-gusoku* (modern armour) were called the *nuinobe-do* and the *mogami-do*. The nuinobe-do was of two-piece construction, hinged at the left, and the horizontal plates usually had their upper edges finished in a series of semi-circles. The horizontal plates of the mogami-do were usually flanged on their upper edge, while the whole do was often of five-piece construction, hinged in four places, giving it the appearance of a jointed box.

Kebiki-odoshi was not entirely forgotten, and some was used in small quantities for decoration. An unusual 'mongrel' style of armour was the *dangaiye-do*, consisting of a do half and half *kebiki* and *nuinobe*.

Once the use of firearms became established the armourers were faced with a further challenge to their art. The result was the *okegawa-do*. This style, somewhat resembling European armour, included a solid-plate do. The horizontal plates were riveted to those above and below them instead of being

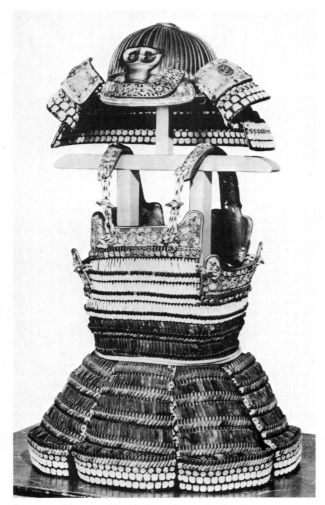

Armour of *haramaki* style (opening at the back).

general term for the body of an armour) would tend to retain a spear point aimed at it, rather than allowing it to glide off harmlessly.

The response of the armour-makers to the above considerations was to result in a number of different styles of armour that were widely used in the Momoyama Period. First, the numerous scales were replaced by solid strips, either made from one piece of metal or from scales riveted together rather than laced. Also, the amount of suspensory lacing was cut down drastically, resulting in the style known as *sugake-odoshi*, whereby the suspensory cords were spaced in pairs; or the even simpler *hishiniu*, which had the horizontal plates fastened one to another by a spaced row of cross knots. The kusazuri (short pieces) were also reduced in size, and in the new styles were symmetrical about the

Two styles of *tosei-gusoku* (modern armour): the *tachi-do* and the *mogami-do*.

laced, producing a surface that, it was hoped, would stop arquebus balls as well as arrows. There were two main variations, depending on how the individual plates were fastened together, either horizontally (*yokohagi-do*) or vertically (*tatehagi-do*). The finest tatehagi-do were the varieties invented by Myochin Hisaie (1573–1615), who lived in Yukinoshita, from which the style takes its name. The *yukinoshita-do* has a smooth surface devoid of any unnecessary lacing, an ideal surface to deflect missiles. So confident were the makers of its efficiency, that they proudly supplied examples which had been tested by having arquebus balls fired at them. The greatest compliment paid to the yukinoshita-do came when Date Masamune (1566–1636) appointed an armourer to make this style for his entire army, the only difference between the highest and lowest ranks being in the finish and the mounting.

One variety of the okegawa-do that also proved immensely popular was the *hotoke-do*. Here the joints between the plates were concealed, or dispensed with altogether by using one large plate, to produce a completely smooth, rounded surface.

The smooth surface of the hotoke-do was an invitation to an artistic armour-maker to add decoration, either in the form of lacquer or by embossing. The latter (*uchidashi-do*) had to be done with care lest it weaken the armour, a fact brought out by an extant specimen dating from 1681 which bears an embossed figure and the proud inscription: '. . . not of thin metal . . . carefully forged using a divine method of forging against arrows and guns by which it is not pierced. Because of this it is a treasure for brave warriors of a military family.'

An important feature of life in Momoyama times was the increased intercourse with Europe. Much trade was carried out, particularly with the Portuguese, and it is not surprising that features of European armour turn up in Japanese styles. One aspect of European armour that was adopted became the *hatomune-do*, or pigeon-breasted cuirass, with a definite central medial line and ridge. Some specimens of Japanese armour actually incorporate pieces from European suits within them, or have parts copied so well as to be almost indistinguishable. For example a sharp-fronted Spanish cuirass might have kusazuri fitted to it, while its accompanying morion helmet would have a neckguard

and peak added, curiously enough after turning the helmet back to front.

One strange design, basically a hammered hotoke-do, were the suits of armour that had the breastplate and backplate beaten into the shape of a naked human body, usually that of an aged monk, with protruding ribs and spine and pendulous breasts.

Momoyama armour was by no means as colourful as older styles, largely because the kebiki-odoshi

Armour of *nuinobe-do* style.

had provided most of the colour. The armour itself was usually lacquered black, brown or finished with russet iron (a form of controlled rusting producing a semi-gloss finish). Less frequently found were red lacquer and gold lacquer. The former was used particularly by the Ii family who dressed all their troops in it, the colour being a bright brick-red, with a deep and glowing finish. The lacing was often dark blue or cornflower blue, with a dash of colour sometimes added by lacing the extreme edge cords of a *sugake* laced plate in 'woodpecker braid' a multicoloured thread on white. Red lacquered armour might be laced with ochre, and gold with white.

Thus the armour of the Momoyama Period was essentially practical. It was robust, efficient and simple, and it may be said that in the Momoyama Period the craft of the armourer reached its peak in the aim of providing the samurai with a suit of armour that would allow him to move about as freely as possible while providing him with the maximum protection against arrow, blade and ball.

The samurai's complete defensive costume would consist of the body armour (the do and kusazuri described above) plus a number of other pieces to protect other parts of the body. Together they made up a suit of armour that was, wherever possible, of complementary style and colour in its constituent parts. Illustrations on pages 25 to 27 show a samurai of the Momoyama Period arming himself. He begins with the fundoshi, or loincloth. It was made of white linen or cotton, a lined variety being worn in winter. He would then put on his *shitagi*, or shirt. The shitagi was similar to the ordinary kimono worn in civilian dress, but shorter. It was buttoned at the breast and tied at the waist with an *obi* (belt). This was wound round twice and tied at the front.

The *kobakama*, as the name implies, were a short version of the hakama trousers worn out of armour. They were narrower than hakama, and of a length that would reach to about five inches below the knee. The samurai would put his left leg in first, then tie in succession the back cords and the front cords, tying both pairs in front.

Our samurai now sits down to put on his tabi, a pair of divided socks in a style still worn today. The recommended material was quilted cotton, and it is recorded that red socks were regarded as being effeminate! A pair of *kiahan* (gaiters) were then wrapped round the calves, taking in the legs of the trousers. The reason for the divided socks becomes apparent when the samurai puts on his next item of equipment, which is his *waraji*, or straw sandals. The sandals had a woven sole and two fixed thongs which passed between the big toe and the second toe. Around the sole were a number of loops, through which another thong would be threaded and fastened. An extra tie under the instep was recommended when marching on steep, snowy or muddy roads, or crossing swamps or rivers. The samurai would always carry a spare pair of sandals, or get someone else to carry them for him.

While still seated the samurai would put on his first item of actual armour, the *suneate*, or shin-guards. The most common form used at this time are illustrated on page 28. They consisted of a number of vertical metal plates joined by chain mail on a cloth backing, with a leather patch on the inside of each to prevent rubbing against the stirrup when riding.

Protection for the thigh was afforded in the form of *haidate*. The haidate looked rather like a divided apron having the lower parts covered with small overlapping plates of metal or leather. They fastened at the waist, and some varieties had in addition ties to fasten the two sections behind the thighs to prevent them swinging up. As the haidate was essentially an item for a mounted samurai it was sometimes discarded for foot fighting, particularly when there was fierce hand-to-hand combat. They could also be awkward when crossing a swamp, so that on the march the haidate were put on normally but with their tying cords fastened outside the body of the do so that they could be removed and replaced easily.

The *yugake* (gloves) were made of tanned skin, sometimes decorated with a pattern. The right-hand glove was always put on first.

There were many different styles of *kote*, or armoured sleeve, but all followed the basic idea of a cloth bag to which were fitted chain mail and metal plates. The chain mail was almost invariably lacquered black, the metal plates being lacquered the same colour as the rest of the armour. A long tying cord passed up through the kote along the

Continued on page 28

24

1 Takeda Shingen, c. 1570
2 Uesugi Kenshin, c. 1570
3 Ashigaru with Kenshin's
 war banners, c. 1570

RICHARD HOOK

A

1 **Kuroda Nagasama, c. 1592**
2 **Samurai with naginata, c. 1590**

B

1 Ashigaru bowman, c. 1576-1615
2 Ashigaru with straw rain-cape, c. 1576-1615
3 Ashigaru arquebusier, c. 1576-1615

2

3

1

RICHARD HOOK

C

1 Tokugawa Ieyasu, battle of Sekigahara, 1600
2 Honda Tadakatsu, battle of Sekigahara, 1600
3 Ashigaru of Tokugawa daimyate, c. 1600

1

2

D

1 & 2 Ashigaru cooking rice in helmet, c. 1600

RICHARD HOOK

E

1 **Date Masamune, siege of Osaka castle, 1615**
2 **Ii Naotaka, siege of Osaka castle, 1615**

RICHARD HOOK

1 **Young samurai**, c. 1600-1700
2 **Old samurai**, c. 1600-1700
3 **Ronin**, c. 1600-1700

RICHARD HOOK

G

1 Maeda Toshiie, c. 1598
2 Kato Kiyomasa, c. 1598

H

結褌帶

被襯衣

紫衣帶

服股衣

履韤子 穿脚絆

乾草鞋

著脇當

Putting on armour, from loincloth to *suneate* (shin guards).

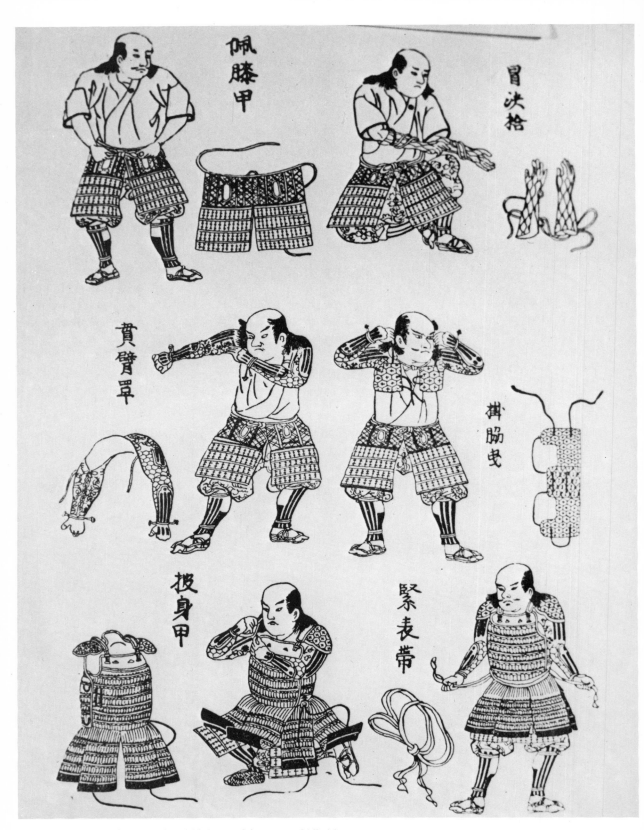

佩膝甲

冒決拾

貫臂羃

掛脇曳

投身甲

緊表帶

Putting on armour, from *haidate* **(thigh guards) to** *uwa-obi* **(belt)**

Putting on armour, from *sode* (shoulder guards) to *kabuto* (helmet).

27

A pair of *haidate* (thigh guards) and one *suneate* (shin guard)—the tying cords on the latter are missing.

A pair of *kote* (armour sleeves), showing tying cords.

continued from page 24

inside of the arm. Some were made with the sleeves joined together, others fastened on to toggles on the do, and some tied on the chest. Sometimes they were made in one with the *wakibiki*, which were pads of cloth and/or chain mail that protected the arm pits.

The samurai would now put on the main part of his armour, the do, with kusazuri attached. Whatever the style of do, the means of attachment was broadly the same. It was suspended from the shoulders by toggles, via the *kohire*, or epaulettes, pads sewn into hexagonal patterns that cushioned the weight of the do on the shoulders, and tied on the right, or in the case of a haramaki, behind the back. The weight would rest on the hips, cushioned by the belt already referred to. After seeing that the do was comfortable, another belt, the *uwa-obi*, would now be tied tightly round the waist.

The samurai was now fully armoured up to the level of his neck. At this point he would put on his *sode*, or shoulder guards, should he be wearing any. Improved styles of do and kote had rendered the sode rather superfluous. The yukinoshita-do, for example, had two metal semi-circular plates that adequately protected the top of the kote. When sode were worn they were usually small and slightly curved, lined inside with cloth down to the level of the lowest plate.

Before arming above the neck the samurai would fit his weapons, which would normally consist of a sword (*katana*) and a dagger (*tanto*). It was unusual for the samurai to wear the short sword when armoured. There were various ways of attaching the sword, either by thrusting through the belt and fastening by means of the silken cord on the scabbard, or suspending it *tachi*-style from the belt, cutting edge downwards.

The base of the throat was protected by a *nodowa*, or throat-guard, which comprised a few metal plates connected by cords. Before putting on his face-mask or *mempo*, the samurai would tie round his head a headcloth or *hachimaki*, which acted as a cushion for the helmet. It was usually about five feet long and traditionally white. To put on the hachimaki the samurai would untie his hair (the example in the illustration has already done so) and comb it back, put the hachimaki at the back of his head, wind it round, and tuck the ends under.

The face-mask (mempo) is one of the most recognizable features of Japanese armour. It varied in style from a simple metal plate shaped to fit the chin, a *hoate*, to a real mask for the whole face (the *somen*). The often-found mempo was a half mask consisting of cheeks, chin and nose-piece, with a hole for the mouth. The mask was traditionally lacquered red inside, and had a small hole so that the sweat could run out. As it had the function of serving as a secure base for fixing the helmet cords, hooks were attached round which the cords could be twisted. The mask was often given features and moustaches.

If the armour of the Momoyama Period was of sombre design, in the helmet, at least, the samurai could express his personality. As if in contrast to the uniformity of styles of the do, the Momoyama Period spawned some weird and wonderful individual creations. The basic helmet (*kabuto*) consisted of a bowl (*hachi*) with a neckguard (*shikoro*) attached, which was made in the same way as the rest of the armour plate. The bowl itself was of many different styles. A simple and popular version was the *zunari*, round, robust and with good reflecting surfaces. The peak of the helmet was lacquered red inside so that its reflection on the samurai's face might make him appear more fearsome.

The extravagant helmet styles arose when a simple helmet bowl was built up into something grotesque, often with the addition of wood and paper only. A good example is Kato Kiyomasa's *naga-eboshi no kabuto*, whose elaborate crown, painted silver and with a red sun on each side, was of paper on a wooden framework. Similar were the 'catfish tails'—gold for Maeda Toshiie (1538–99) and silver in that of Hori Hidemasa (1553–90). One variation, that looked most effective when worn in conjunction with the style of armour made to look like a human body, was the 'hairy helmet', with horse hair combed to look like a head of hair, and sometimes a pigtail and even a pair of pink ears added for effect.

Yamamoto Kansuke, a retainer of Takeda Shingen, had a helmet fitted with large buffalo horns of wood. A similar one was worn by Kuroda Nagamasa (1568–1623), who had another oddly shaped helmet called an *ichi-no-tani kabuto*. It took its name from a famous battle in 1184 when the samurai Minamoto Yoshitsune led his army down a steep cliff. The shape of the helmet was supposed to reproduce the sweep of the cliff. Honda Tadakatsu (1548–1610) wore a pair of stylized wooden antlers. Ii Naomasa and his son Naotaka

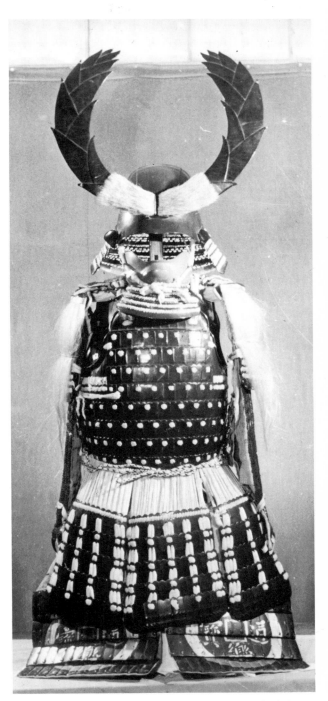

Armour of *nuinobe-do* style, with a *zunari*-style helmet, ornamented with an elaborate frontlet.

29

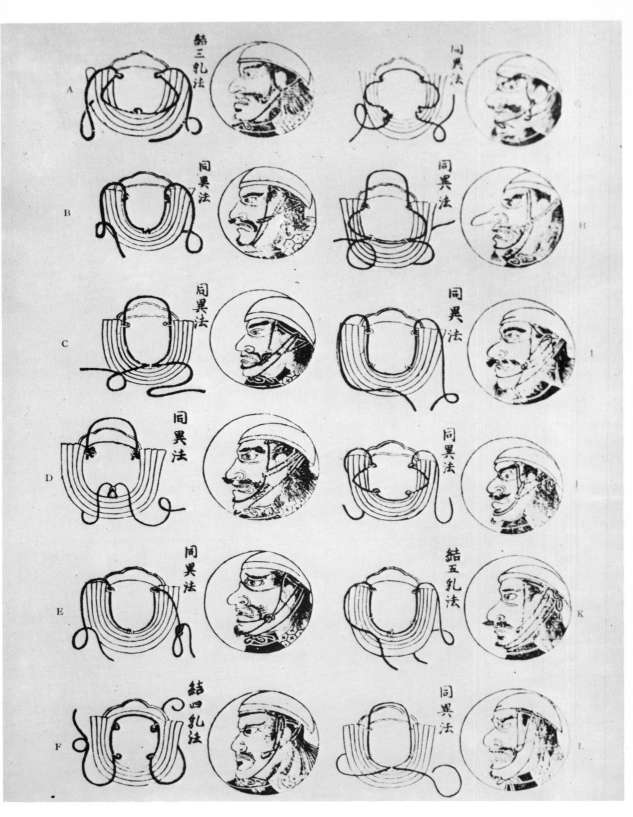

Various ways of attaching the helmet cords.

wore *zunari kabuto* to which were added gilded metal horns and horse-hair plumes.

Alternatively a basic helmet could be adorned by means of various badges. Date Masamune (1566–1636) favoured an asymmetrical golden crescent moon, and smaller ones were worn by his samurai. Toyotomi Hideyoshi (1536–98) wore a huge sunburst crest at the back of one of his helmets. Tokugawa Ieyasu added a beautiful golden fern-leaf crest to the front of several plain helmets.

The helmet was fastened securely by means of a long cord, usually red or blue regardless of the colour of the rest of the armour lacing. The illustration on page 30 shows how this was done.

The samurai was now ready for battle, but with all the uniformity of armour, which would extend to the helmet for an ordinary samurai, some means was needed of proclaiming one's identity to friend and foe. This need was satisfied by the *sashimono*, an identifying device worn on the back. More often than not the sashimono was a small vertical flag bearing the mon or badge of the wearer if he was of sufficient rank, or of his master if he was not, but many other things, such as feathers and various three-dimensional objects, were used. To attach the sashimono, which was fixed on a pole, the do carried a socket in the small of the back, and at the level of the shoulder blades a hinged bridge piece. These held the wooden holder into which the sashimono fitted. It must have been somewhat awkward to wear, and there is pictorial evidence that for high-ranking samurai at least the foot-soldiers performed the service of removing the sashimono and holding it while their superior engaged in hand-to-hand combat.

Several accessory items of equipment need to be mentioned. On some do's there is a small cloth pocket. This is for a handkerchief, but may well have been used to carry other things. Sometimes a leather patch would be worn on the left of the do to stop the sword scabbard rubbing. Various other items include a towel, a provision bag, a bag in which to carry one's enemy's severed head, a purse, a hooked rope, a coil of rope and a medicine case. The rope and bags could be attached to the saddle when riding, but in most cases samurai would have servants to carry these things for them.

When not actually fighting, the samurai liked to wear a *jinbaori,* a long ornamental surcoat worn over armour. It was often beautifully embroidered, particularly on the back. Maeda Toshiie's wife embroidered her husband's jinbaori with a picture of Shoki, the mythological queller of demons.

A bizarre item of equipment was the *horo*, which looked like a cloth balloon and consisted of a cloak stretched over a framework. Its original function was to act as an 'arrow catcher', but by the Momoyama Period it had become purely ceremonial.

Precisely how much of the armour described above was actually worn at any given time would depend on the circumstances. The mask and haidate could be omitted for fierce close fighting, and the shinguards, too, might be discarded if the enemy occupied higher ground. There was not always time to put on the suit of armour in the laborious way described above. If a samurai was caught unawares he could pull his do on quickly if it was placed on an armour chest or suspended from the ceiling. In such a case it would be advantageous to have already attached the sleeves to the do.

Samurai who were also monks, such as the famous Takeda Shingen and Uesugi Kenshin, could wear the Buddhist monk's *kesa* over their armour, under the surcoat. The kesa was rather like a shawl, with an ivory ring on the left side. It is illustrated on page 32. Uesugi Kenshin is usually represented pictorially without a helmet but wearing a monk's white head-cowl.

During the Momoyama Period no armour was made for the horse. Instead the animal would often be gaily decked with long braid tassels. The saddle was of lacquered wood, and the strangely shaped stirrups of iron. When on campaign the horse would be used to carry various necessities, such as a bag of rice for the samurai and fodder for the horse. These bags would be fastened to the saddle. In the Edo Period, when matchlock pistols were developed, a pair could be carried in leather holsters. In camp the horse was tethered by a rope, and prevented from moving by a silken band wrapped round its front legs. Decorative items which were often observed were large ornamental saddle cloths, embroidered with mon or made from animal skins. Horseshoes were not worn at this time, and it is an interesting point of detail that the samurai mounted his horse from the right.

Hojo Soun (1432–1519) wearing a monk's *kesa* (ritual scarf).

Dress and Equipment: Ashigaru

The increasing recognition of the importance of the lower-class warrior in the Momoyama Period led to an increased concern for his dress and protection. Yamagata Masakage, one of Takeda Shingen's ablest generals, was to recognize early the effect of uniformity on an enemy, and used to select any of his samurai who happened to be wearing red armour and put them in the front rank. This idea was later copied by Ii Naomasa, who went so far as to dress his entire army in red.

The daimyo would supply his ashigaru with armour and helmet, but the soldier would be expected to provide his own swords. The need to mass-produce vast quantities of basic armour led to the introduction of what was effectively the first military uniform in Japan.

The ashigaru would first put on a simple loincloth. The shirt, too, would be simple, extending as far as the hips, and with short sleeves. It would be tucked into a pair of close-fitting trousers that extended as far as the ankles and looked rather like 'long johns'. He may have worn tabi socks in the winter, but otherwise his feet would be left bare. The straw sandals were identical to those worn by samurai, and kiahan (gaiters) would sometimes be worn. The shirt and trousers were pulled tight with a belt, into which the ashigaru would thrust his wakizashi, or short sword. Later in our period, when the definition of samurai became more precise and the division was made complete between warriors and farmers, the ashigaru became officially low-grade samurai and could wear the two swords that were the hallmark of the class.

The ashigaru's hair was let down, combed, and covered with the hachimaki as was the samurai's. His kote sleeves were, however, much simpler, unless an ashigaru could augment his standard issue armour by wearing a pair he had purchased or found on a battlefield. The standard issue were little more than a cloth bag with metal plates attached. The do was of course much simpler than the elaborate samurai styles. It was usually of two-piece construction as a simple okegawa-do. The front and back were usually each of one plate. An exception were the ashigaru of Date Masamune, all of whom wore basic versions of the yukinoshita-do.

Several illustrations indicate the use of mon of the lord to distinguish the ashigaru of his army. The mon was applied in gold or red lacquer on the front and back of the do.

The ashigaru helmet was known as a *jingasa*, or war hat. It was commonly made from metal or toughened leather, and often had the shape of a flat cone. Tokugawa Ieyasu recommended a light iron one, so that the ashigaru could cook their rice in it! It had a padded, detachable lining, and fastened with two cords attached to two padded loops. In many cases the mon that appeared on the do would be repeated on the jingasa. A variation on the conical shape was the *shingen* style, named after Takeda Shingen, which was curved and had a turned-up peak. To protect against sun and rain, the jingasa had a cloth hanging down to the shoulders from its rim.

Unlike the samurai, the ashigaru was expected to

carry all his needs on his person. The rations were carried in a dozen small cloth bags tied together, each individual bag holding the rice for one meal. This rope of bags was slung in front of the arms and across the back. In addition the ashigaru would have a utility bag, which was tied by a flap and cord and carried round the waist, hanging at the back and fastening at the front. The list of contents makes interesting reading. It includes paper, medicines, pickled plums, antidotes to poison, money, writing brushes, a small knife and a length of cord. One authority recommends the ashigaru to carry with him in cold weather a few red peppers to nibble if he feels chilly.

Unarmoured servants (wakato) and pages (komono) would wear similar clothes except for the do and kote. Instead they would wear a short kimono, and their only defensive armour would be a jingasa.

Any other equipment an ashigaru carried would depend on which specialist corps he belonged to:

Archers

The Japanese bow, being originally designed with the mounted archer in mind, was of unusual construction in that although it was a longbow it was actually fired from a hand grip one-third of the way up the shaft. The bow was made of lengths of bamboo and other woods glued together, lacquered, and bound with rattan. It required great strength to pull, one reason why the firearm was becoming increasingly popular. The quiver was carried on the right hip. Again, this was a different design from its Western counterpart. The most popular quiver at this time was one in which the arrows were enclosed within a box, either lacquered or covered in fur, which protected the flights from the effects of weather. The arrows were withdrawn through a 'door' where the points of the arrows fitted, and brought round to be fired from the right-hand side of the bow, rather than over the shoulder to the left, Western style. A spare bowstring was carried on a basketwork reel attached on the left side to the cord that held the quiver. As each quiver held only two dozen arrows, further supplies were available from an arrow-bearer, who bore a giant 100-arrow quiver on his back. When firing the bow it was considered more convenient to remove the jingasa.

Spearmen

Two types of pole-arm were used by the Japanese at this time. The naginata had been used for centuries. It was a form of glaive, with a blade about the same length as the wakizashi, or short sword, mounted on a long shaft. Far more popular were *yari*—spears of various lengths with straight blades. Some had very short blades like those in a tanto dagger, others were long and straight. Some had cross-blades fitted on one side or both, by means of which an ashigaru could catch a horseman and dismount him, in order to finish him off with the straight portion. A long spear was the accepted weapon of a samurai, which he would wield standing up in the saddle, swinging the spear

Typical *do* (body armour) worn by an ashigaru, bearing the *mon* (badge) of the Satake daimyo.

Flag of *nobori* style used by Takeda Shingen, bearing the legend: 'Steady as a mountain, attack like fire, still as a wood, swift as the wind' in gold characters on blue.

from side to side. A well-made spear had the tang of the blade sunk deep into the shaft, which was ideally of seasoned oak, lacquered, with metal decorations where the tang fitted, and with a metal ferrule. When not in use the blade would be protected by a scabbard.

Arquebusiers

By the end of the Momoyama Period the arquebusier had become the most important ashigaru in the samurai army. He was armed with a *teppo*, as the Japanese called the gun, which was a firearm which worked on the matchlock principle, whereby a lighted match was dropped on to the priming powder in the touch-hole which set off the main charge in the barrel. The barrel was made of iron, and fitted neatly into a wooden stock, the ramrod being carried underneath.

The gun would be loaded with powder and ball, and a little priming powder introduced into the touch-hole which was then closed with a brass cover to guard against premature discharge. The smouldering match, carried round the ashigaru's left forearm (about six feet was required to keep the match alight all day), was inserted into the 'S'-shaped lever called the serpentine, which was cocked by pulling back against an external brass spring. The ashigaru blew the match into glowing life, the brass safety plate was opened, and a pull on the trigger dropped the spluttering match down on to the touch-hole.

The gunpowder was carried in a flask on the right side, and balls in a small leather bag. Further supplies of both were obtainable from the ammunition-bearer, who carried them in a stout reinforced box on his back. Some illustrations depict arquebusiers with what are clearly spare ramrods carried over their backs. Ramrods were of wood, and to break one would put a teppo out of action until it could be replaced.

A ramrod was used as a 'swagger stick' by the *teppo ko-gashira*, the officer in charge of a teppo group. By indicating with his ramrod, the officer would dress the ranks and give the signal to fire. The ramrod was sometimes carried inside a length of bamboo. The normal size of a teppo group was between thirty and fifty men, with one *ko-gashira* per ten men. On the march the arquebus could be slung across the back by the cord the ashigaru carried in his utility bag, or slung from the waist in a bag or lacquered waterproof case.

Other corps
The most important rôle in the subsidiary corps was the carrying of food. Food was carried for the whole army, except for the vanguard when the army was advancing, who would be expected to live off the land. Some food was carried on men's backs, but the bulk was carried by pack horses, each horse being led by a wakato servant. The packs were made of bundles of rice straw, and each horse carried two with a little flag for identification. Wheeled transport was never properly developed in medieval Japan, largely owing to the mountainous terrain over which most travelling had to be done, so there were no supply wagons such as were found in contemporary European armies.

The sandal-bearer was effectively the samurai's batman, and as well as carrying the sandals would usually carry a box bearing the lord's personal necessities.

A number of footsoldiers would always be seen clustered round the general on a field of battle. All had duties connected in some way with communications. Audible signals were given by means of drums, gongs, bells and the *horogai*, a trumpet made out of a large conch shell, fitted with a mouthpiece and with cords for carrying. One ashigaru would be in charge of the conch. Two would be deputed to handle the drum, one to carry it on his back, and the other to beat it. The drums varied from quite simple ones carried by two shoulderstraps to large affairs mounted on a decorative wooden stand, bearing a mon on the drumskin. Gongs and bells were of bronze, and were not usually carried round but were set in a fixed position near the headquarters. They were used for summoning, and informing the army of the time of day.

A very large number of ashigaru would have the jobs of carrying flags. Flags and banners had been used for centuries, largely in the form of the *hata-jirushi*, or streamer, a long rectangular flag supported on a narrow crosspiece at the top of a long pole. It usually bore the owner's mon. The 16th century introduced a variation on this style called the *nobori*, whereby the crosspiece of the hata-jirushi was attached at one end to the top of the shaft,

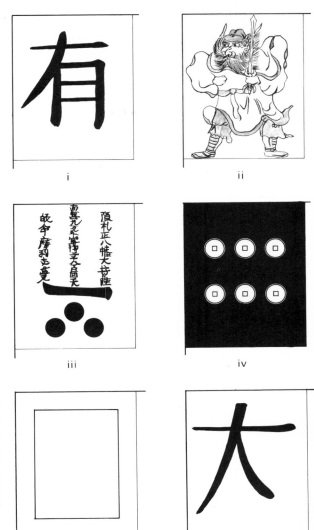

Shihan (rectangular flag) versions of the *uma-jirushi* (standard): (i) The character 'yu' in black on white; used by Hosokawa Tadaoki (1564–1645). (ii) Shoki the demon queller, black on white, used by Maeda Toshiie (1538–99). (iii) An invocation of Hachiman the war god, over the *mon* of the Mori family, used by them from c. 1555–1615. Black on white. (iv) Flag used by Sanada Yukimura (1570–1615) White on black. (v) White rectangle on gold. Used by Oda Nobutada (1557–82). (vi) 'Dai' meaning 'great', used by Takeda Katsuyori (1546–82).

and the whole of one side of the flag was fastened along the shaft's length. This gave a rigid flag that would flutter a little in the wind but would still maintain its shape and could be read easily.

One purpose of a flag was to indicate the whereabouts of a general, and so as the nobori became popular, and the same flags tended to appear everywhere the eye could see, a new device was introduced called the *uma-jirushi*, which

A wounded samurai, bearing the severed heads of his enemies.

literally means horse insignia. 'Standard' is probably the most meaningful interpretation. Many generals had two, the *o-uma-jirushi* (great standard) and the *ko-uma-jirushi* (lesser standard). One instantly recognizable example was the great standard of Tokugawa Ieyasu, which flew at every battle in which he fought following his adoption of it in 1566. It consisted of a giant golden fan made of strengthened paper, mounted on wooden spines five feet long, and raised on a fifteen-foot-high shaft. A red rising sun was painted on each side. For his lesser standard he used a bronze disc pierced with a circular hole at the top. Besides these he had seven nobori of white cloth with three Tokugawa mon on each. Before leaving northern Japan for the Battle of Sekigahara in 1600 he gave these banners to his heir Hidetada and carried plain ones with him.

One other flag was a treasure of the Tokugawa house. It was a white hata-jirushi which bore on it the slogan 'Renounce this filthy world and attain the Pure Land', referring to the Jodo or Pure Land sect of Buddhism, by whom the flag had been presented to Ieyasu's ancestor.

The other cognizances used by the Tokugawa were the mon painted on the armour of the ashigaru, and the use of the character go (meaning five) on the sashimono of the élite utsukai-ban, the 'honourable messenger corps'.

Many objects appeared as uma-jirushi. Oda Nobunaga sported a colossal red umbrella. Toyotomi Hideyoshi used a large wooden gourd painted gold. He is supposed to have added a gourd for every victory he won, until by the time of his death the standard was known as the 'thousand gourd'— metaphorically if not literally.

A large rectangular flag or *shihan* was a popular form of uma-jirushi. The Ii clan, whose use of red has already been noted, used a large red flag with the first character of their name on it in gold. Their lesser standard was a golden cone with red streamers. Maeda Toshiie had one with a picture of 'Shoki' the demon queller. Three generations of Mori samurai bore one with an invocation of Hachiman the war god.

The lesser standard, nobori, and hata-jirushi were all usually light enough to be carried by one man. They could be fitted into a leather pocket tied at the waist, or slotted into a specially strengthened

A samurai in *kimono* with close-fitting trousers. His hair is worn in the *chasen-gami* (tea-whisk) style.

and padded sashimono-holder on the back. If the nobori was long, or the day was blustery, it was advantageous to run a cord from the top of it to the soldier's hand to control it. The hata-jirushi was found easier to control if it was carried at the front. The great standard would probably be mounted on a framework on the ground where the general had established his headquarters. If it was necessary to move it about, it would be fixed on one soldier's back while two others held the strings from the top. As well as indicating the general's position the standards also served as a rallying point. When things were going badly for Ieyasu at the Battle of Mikata-ga-hara in 1572 he planted his fan standard on high ground to rally his troops.

* * *

The Plates

Two flags of Takeda Shingen, both red, with gold Chinese characters and black *bonji* (Sanskrit characters).

A1 Takeda Shingen, c. 1570

Takeda Shingen (1521–73) is dressed as he would have appeared at one of the many battles of Kawanakajima. His *do-maru* is ornamented with his personal *mon*. His simple multiplate helmet is set off with a horsehair plume, wooden horns, and a devil's face. Over his armour he wears a Buddhist *kesa*, and a half-sleeved version of the *jinbaori*. A conservative in his dress, Shingen wears an old-fashioned *do-maru* and bearskin boots.

A2 Uesugi Kenshin, c. 1570

Shingen's celebrated adversary, Uesugi Kenshin (1530–78) was also a monk, and has adopted the monkish head cowl in place of a helmet.

A3 Ashigaru with Kenshin's war banners, c. 1570

These foot soldiers wear very simple armours consisting of metal plates joined by strips of chain mail on a cloth backing; their only head protection is a piece of mail sewn to a *hachimaki*. They are dressed as for a summer campaign. The banner on the left bears the character 'ryo' (dragon), and that on the right is 'bi', the first character in the name of Bishamon-ten, one of Japan's three war-gods.

B1 Kuroda Nagasama, c. 1592

Kuroda Nagasama (1568–1623) was the commander of the third division of the Japanese army which invaded Korea in 1592. He wears a *hishiniu-do* with *kusazuri* laced in *kebiki-odoshi*. His helmet is an *ichi-no-tani kabuto*.

B2 Samurai with naginata, c. 1590

This samurai is wearing one of the most remarkable styles of armour developed in Japan: it is basically a *hotoke-do*, hammered and lacquered to resemble a human torso. The back of the *do* would show the shape of the spine. The 'hair' on the helmet is horsehair, combed back into a pigtail in the samurai style.

C1 Ashigaru bowman, c. 1576–1615

The foot soldiers who comprised the bulk of the armies of the larger and better organized *daimyo* from about 1576 onwards were issued with simple

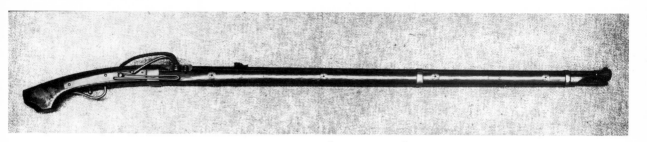

Japanese arquebus.

okegawa-do such as that illustrated here; all features of the armour are of basic design. The archer has removed his *jingasa* to facilitate drawing his bow.

C2 Ashigaru spearman, c. 1576–1615

The spear (*yari*) was the standard polearm for the *ashigaru*. This soldier is wearing a rice-straw rain cape over his armour.

C3 Ashigaru arquebusier, c. 1576–1615

This shows the *jingasa* clearly. Note the *mon* of the Satake daimyate on the *do* and the *jingasa*. Around his shoulders and back are slung his ration bags.

D1 Tokugawa Ieyasu, battle of Sekigahara, 1600

The great Tokugawa Ieyasu (1542–1616), victor of Sekigahara, is shown here seated as if about to commence the viewing of the heads of the slain. He is wearing the *namban-do* which he is supposed to have worn at that battle. The armour and helmet were of Spanish manufacture, with modifications and additions to satisfy Japanese taste. He holds his *saihai* in his right hand.

D2 Honda Tadakatsu, battle of Sekigahara, 1600

Honda Tadakatsu (1548–1610) was Ieyasu's companion in all his campaigns. He wears a *nuinobe-do* laced in *sugake-odoshi*, with a very large Buddhist rosary slung round his body. His helmet is strikingly ornamented with lacquered wooden antlers. Behind him is the screen or *maku*, bearing the Tokugawa *mon*, and above it may be seen the *o-uma-jirushi*.

D3 Ashigaru of Tokugawa daimyate, 1600

These are dressed identically to those in Plate C apart from the Tokugawa *mon*. The left hand banner is a *hata-jirushi*, bearing the *Jodo* motto, 'Renounce this filthy world and attain the Pure Land'. The other is a *nobori* with three Tokugawa *mon*.

E1 Ashigaru, and E2 Wakato, c. 1576–1615

The *ashigaru* is about to add some ingredient from his utility bag, normally carried at the small of the back, to the meal he is cooking in his up-turned *jingasa*. On his head he wears a large *hachimaki*, and his *shitagi* and trousers are clearly seen. The *wakato* wears no armour but the *jingasa*, and a short kimono. He is opening one of a set of ration bags. The baggage train in the background, led by *ashigaru* and *wakato*, carries packs made from bundles of rice straw, with little flags as identification.

F1 Date Masamune, siege of Osaka castle, 1615

Date Masamune (1566–1636), whose most renowned physical feature was a staring and damaged left eyeball, is shown here wearing a *yukinoshita-do*, the style of armour with which he equipped all his retainers. His large *sashimono* bears the rising sun.

F2 Ii Naotaka, siege of Osaka castle, 1615

Ii Naotaka (1590–1659), who also fought at Osaka, equipped his army, down to the lowest *ashigaru*, with red armour. His own is a *dangaiye-do* with a *zunari-kabuto* with large gold *kuwagata*. In the background siege constructions can be seen by the keep of Osaka castle.

G1 and G2 Young and old samurai, c. 1600–1700

A young samurai and an older relative in everyday dress are confronted by a *ronin* in quarrelsome mood. The young man, whose age is indicated by his hairstyle, is wearing *kamishimo*—i.e., *kataginu* and *hakama*; the latter shows the heavy folds taken by the material during storage. The older man, bald naturally rather than by artifice, wears similar costume, with the same *mon* on garments of different colours.

G3 Ronin, c. 1600–1700

The ronin's appearance indicates his outcast status. He has completely neglected his hairdressing, and wears one old armour sleeve as protection. He is, however, ready for action, having discarded his scabbard, tied up his sleeves with the *tasuki*, and tied his *ko-bakama* tightly about him.

H1 Maeda Toshiie, c. 1598

Maeda Toshiie (1538–99) wore this stunning gold-lacquered armour laced in white. His helmet is decorated with white horsehair over the *shikoro*. The armour is a *mogami-do*.

H2 Kato Kiyomasa, c. 1598

In front of his creation, Kumamoto Castle, sits Kato Kiyomasa, on the skin of a tiger—perhaps the beast which he slew in North Korea in 1593 in a well-known incident. He wears a finely ornamented *jinbaori*, and his well-known *naga-eboshi-no-kabuto*, which he is known to have worn during the Korean War.

Notes sur les planches en couleur

A1 Takeda Shingen habillé comme il l'aurait été lors d'une des batailles à Kawanakajima. Son *do-maru* porte son *mon* personnel et par dessus son armure il porte une kesa bouddhique et un *jinbaori* à demi-manches. **A2** Uesugi Kenshin, l'ennemi célèbre de Shingen, était également moine et a adopté ici le capuchon du moine au lieu d'un casque. **A3** Les *ashigaru*—soldats d'infanterie—tiennent les bannières de guerre de Shingen; à gauche le caractère *ryo*, à droite, le *bi*.

B1 Kuroda Nagasama, le commandant de la troisième division de l'armée japonaise qui avait envahi la Corée en 1592, porte un *hishiniu-do* avec un *kusazuri* lacé en *kebiki-odoshi*. Le casque est un *ichi-no-tani kabuto*. **B2** Un Samurai portant une *naginata* et vêtu d'une armure extraordinaire du genre *hotoke-do* formée et peinte afin de ressembler à un torse humain nu; son casque est surmonté d'une perruque en crin.

C Des *Ashigaru*, portant tous une armure simple et typique du genre *okegawa*. Le chapeau du mousquetaire (*jingasa*) et l'armure portent le *mon* de la famille Satake. L'homme portant d'une lance a une cape de pluie en paille de riz.

D1 Tokugawa Ieyasu est réputé avoir porté cette armure *namban-do* de fabrication espagnole à la grande bataille de Sekigahara. **D2** Pendant que son seigneur se prépare à inspecter les têtes des massacrés, son fidèle compagnon Honda Tadakatsu se tient prêt. Son armure est une *nuinobe-do*, son casque est surmonté de défenses en bois et il porte en bandoulière un énorme chapelet bouddhique. Le paravent porte le *mon* des Tokugawa. La bannière en forme d'éventail, *o-uma-jirushi*, est visible à l'arrière-plan. **D3** Deux bannières des Tokugawa; celle de gauche du type *hata-jirushi* et porte la devise *Jodo* 'Renonce à ce sale monde et gagne la Terre Pure'. Celle de droite est un *nobori* avec le *mon* des Tokugawa.

E Un *ashigaru* et un *wakato* en train de préparer un repas dont les ingrédients ont été pris dans les sacs à provisions et cuisinés dans un chapeau de guerre renversé.

F1 Date Masamune au siège du château d'Osaka en 1615; notez son oeil gauche au regard fixe! Il équipait ses gens d'armure *yukinoshita-do*. **F2** Ii Naotaka, qui s'est également battu à Osaka, équipait toute son armée d'armure rouge. La sienne est une *dangaiye-do* avec un casque *zunari-kabuto* garni d'une grande *kuwagata* en or.

G Un jeune samurai et un vieux parent, portant le costume quotidien composé d'un *kataginu* et d'une *hakama* portant un *mon* de famille, se trouvent en présence d'un *ronin* exilé. Celui-ci n'a comme protection qu'une seule vieille manche cuirassée. Prévoyant un combat, il a rétréci ses manches et les a attachées avec le *tasuki*.

H1 Maeda Toshiie portait cette armure laquée d'or du type *mogami-do*. **H2** Kato Kiyomasa, le héros de la Guerre de Corée et tueur de tigres, porte un magnifique *jinbaori* et le casque spectaculaire pour lequel il était célèbre, le *naga-eboshi-no-kabuto*.

Farbtafeln

A1 Takeda Shingen, wie er bei einer der Schlachten zu Kawanakajima ausgesehen hätte. Sein *do-maru* ist mit seinem persönlichen *mon* ausgezeichnet und über seinem Harnisch trägt er einen buddhistischen *kesa* und einen halbärmeligen *jinbaori*. **A2** Uesugi Kenshin, Shingens berühmter Feind, war auch ein Mönch und hat sich eine Mönchenkapuze statt einem Helm angeeignet. **A3** *Ashigaru*—Fusssoldaten—tragen Shingens Kriegsfahnen; links das Schriftzeichen *ryo* und rechts *bi*.

B1 Kuroda Nagasama, Kommandeur der dritten Division des japanishen Heeres, das im Jahre 1592 in Korea eingedrungen ist. Er trägt einen in *kebiki-odoshi* geschnürten *hishiniu-do* und *kusazuri*: Der Helm ist ein *ichi-no-tani kabuto*. **B2** Der Samurai trägt in der Hand einen *naginata* und trägt merkwürdigen *hotoke-do* Harnisch, der nach Ähnlichkeit eines nackten menschlichen Oberkörpers gestaltet und bemalen ist mit einer aus Rosshaar hergestellten Perücke auf dem Helm.

C *Ashigaru*, die alle Harnisch des einfachen *okegawa-do* Typs tragen Der Hut (*jingasa*) und Harnisch des Musketiers tragen den *mon* der Satakefamilie. Der Lanzenträger trägt einen aus Reisstroh hergestellten Regenumhang.

D1 Tokugawa Ieyasu soll diesen *namban-do* Harnisch spanischer Herstellung bei der grossen Schlacht zu Sekigahara getragen haben. **D2** Während sein Herr sich die Köpfe der Erschlagenen zu besichtigen vorbereitet steht ihm sein untrennbarer Genosse Honda Tadakatsu zur Seite. Sein Harnisch ist ein *nuinobe-do*, auf seinem Helm trägt er ein holzernes Geweih und einen Körper hängt ein enormer buddhistischer Rosenkranz. Der Schirm trägt den Togukawa *mon*. Die Fächerfahne, *o-uma-jirushi* ist auch zu sehen. **D3** Zwei Tokugawa Fahnen; die Linke ist vom *hata-jirushi* Typ, worauf der Stichwort 'Schwöre diese unreine Welt ab und gelange zum reinen Land' zu lesen ist. Rechts ist ein *nobori* mit dem Tokugawa *mon*.

E *Ashigaru* und *wakato* bereiten das Essen vor. Die Zutaten werden aus den Verpflegungssäcken genommen und in einem umgestülpten eisernen Kriegshut gekocht.

F1 Date Masamune bei der Belagerung von der Festung Osaka im Jahre 1615; bemerkenswert ist sein starrender linker Augapfel; sein ganzes Gefolge hat er mit diesem *yukinoshita-do* Harnisch ausgerüstet. **F2** Ii Naotaka, der auch bei Osaka gekämpft hat, sein ganzes Heer mit rotem Harnisch ausgerüstet. Selbst trägt er einen *dangaiye-do* mit *zunari-kabuto* Helm, der mit einem hohen, goldenen *kuwagata* versehen ist.

G Ein junger Samurai mit seinem älteren Verwandten, die im Alltagsbekleidung von *kataginu* und *hakama* mit Familien*mon* angezogen sind, werden von einem ausgestossenen *ronin* entgegengetreten. Dieser hat nur noch einen gepanzerten Ärmel zum Schutze. Voraussehend, dass es zum Kämpfen kommen könnte, hat er seine Ärmel mit dem *tasuki* hochgebunden.

H1 Maeda Toshiie trug diesen gold lackierten Harnisch. **H2** Kato Kiyomasa, Held des koreanischen Krieges und Erleger von Tigern trägt einen feinen *jinbaori* und den berühmten, auffallenden *naga-eboshi-no-kabuto* Helm.